Candyland

BY

Jeremy Raison

13 Publishing

First published by 13 Publishing in Great Britain, May 2014

Candyland copyright © Jeremy Raison 2014

Jeremy Raison has asserted his right to be identified as the author of this work

ISBN 978-1-909809-06-2

A CIP catalogue record for this book is available from the British Library

Amateur performing rights Applications for performance in excerpt form or in full by non-professionals in English throughout the world should be addressed to 13 Publishing, 169 Mugdock Road, Milngavie, Glasgow G62 8NB (tel: 0141 563 9686). Publication of this play does not necessarily indicate its availability for amateur performance.

Professional performing rights Applications for performance by professionals in any medium and in any language throughout the world should be addressed to 13 Publishing, 169 Mugdock Road, Milngavie, Glasgow G62 8NB (tel: 0141 563 9686). No performance of any kind may be given unless a licence has been obtained. Application should be made before rehearsals begin.

Cover photograph © Sharon Mackenzie

For information on the author: www.jeremyraison.com

JEREMY RAISON

Jeremy Raison is an award-winning author of more than 30 stage plays including **The Rain Gathering** (National Theatre, Traverse), **The Sound of My Voice** (Citizens, Assembly, Made In Scotland), **Blitz** (Traverse, Kirkaldy College), **Charlie and the Chocolate Factory** (Sadlers Wells, Dominion West End, National touring, Denmark, Sweden), **Don Juan** (Citizens), **Heart and Soul** (Chester Gateway), **Wake Me In the Morning** (Oran Mor), **Therese Raquin** (Citizens), **Jumping Jack Flash** (Liverpool Everyman), **Savage Britannia** (National Theatre Studio, Mandela), **A Distant Shore** (National Theatre Studio), **Wee Fairy Tales** (Citizens, national touring), **Once Upon A Time** (Chester Gateway) and **A Child of Europe** (Theatre Workshop).

For radio he has written **The Rain Gathering**, **Music To See By**, **The Readers of Broken Wheel Recommend**, **Cuckoo** and **Eavesdropper** (all Radio 4), **Sam's Secret Orchestra** (Radio 3) and a six hour WW1 project for Amazon Audible.

For film he wrote and directed **Seen** (BBC1).

Jeremy was Artistic Director of the Glasgow Citizens Theatre for seven years during which time the company tripled its box office, was nominated for seventy three awards and toured internationally, as well as to the West End. He also ran Chester Gateway Theatre for four years winning the TMA/Stage Award for Outstanding Achievement in Regional Theatre.

ALSO BY JEREMY RAISON

Wake Me In the Morning
The Rain Gathering
Therese Raquin adapted from Emile Zola
Bring Me Sunshine
The Sound of My Voice adapted from Ron Butlin
Heart and Soul a play with live soul music

CAST

STAR
late 40s

LADY
his girlfriend, mid 30s

CITY
27 years old

SETTING

An aircraft hangar in the middle of the desert

ACT ONE: A DYING GOD

An aircraft hangar full of moth-balled Second World War airplanes, covered in tarpaulins.

In a corner of the hangar - which may be all we see - is a small work shack, and spilling out from this area a table top on trestles, covered in plans: working drawings covered in stains and mugs. There's also a small fridge full of beer, a kettle, a battered sofa, prettified with a few cushions, and a solid red safe, its door facing away from the audience.

Two giant sliding hangar doors lead out to the empty desert.

Star is in full flow.

STAR Zero to airborne in no time, baby! Boy, you gotta feel that power right between your thighs, growl and rush, gotta feel the roar, baby! Fucking dynamite -
LADY I want a house.

STAR These are better'n any house.
LADY That's what this is?
STAR Hey, don't be jealous, baby.
LADY Of these? These hunks of – rust?! Honey, you're delusional.
STAR You are jealous.
LADY Maybe we should be careful who you talk to, unless you want to get yourself certified. These're relics from a bygone age, darling. Hell, they're only here because no one else in their right mind even wants to look at them!

He coughs, a dry cough, ignores it.

STAR You wouldn't understand.
LADY What don't I understand?
STAR You'll get your house.
LADY You need a house too, baby.
STAR These survived a war, they deserve respect -
LADY Please don't tell me this museum is more important than us.
STAR You see a museum? These fly!
LADY These go nowhere.
STAR That's what they do, baby! Fly til they drop.
LADY Why does your use of language not give me comfort?
STAR Hell, you know what I mean, babycakes, quit squeezing my melons.
LADY I know you like to crash things, darling. That's you! You're a one man - you're a wrecking ball, all of your own making! So, please, honey, let's not make this thing worse than it is.
STAR Hey!
LADY OK, tell me what you haven't busted. Let's see: fibia no. Tibia no. Collar bone, no. Three, four ribs, five ribs, who's counting? You punctured a lung as I remember –
STAR All healed now, baby –
LADY Metatarsal busted, neck busted, two vertebrae busted. Just tell me if I'm missing anything out here?
STAR Not in one of these. Up there, sky's all mine. Ain't nothing and no one to hit, I'm free as a buzzard prowling the prairie.
LADY You still have to land, honey. If you ever get one of these ladies off the ground.
STAR Ten to one says I will.
LADY You even have a licence?

LADY Tell me you have your badge, sweetheart.
STAR Think I can't fly, darlin', you're wrong.
LADY Maybe you should learn which way is up, make it easy on yourself.
STAR Look out the goddamm window, won't I!
LADY You'll have to pass me first.

STAR Go out one morning while you're asleep.
LADY I'll hear you. Groping round in the pitch dark for a beer and a flash-light and your pants and God knows what else, honey. I'll hear the engines, won't I?
STAR Too late to stop me.
LADY Don't worry, I'll stop you alright. I'll barricade the doors.
STAR Come with me. Join the mile high club, baby.
LADY Is that all you think of?
STAR That's me. Say it like it is.
LADY These museum pieces know auto-pilot, do they?

STAR I can push buttons. I can make it so a plane flies straight.
LADY OK, you're a genius, lover. So why don't you find yourself a nice little Comanche 250, a twin engine Apache! Better still, pay a guy who knows what he's doing.
STAR Don't want no pilot, baby, don't want nobody else but you.
LADY Honey, it'll take more than a few pretty words to win me round.
STAR Come over here, babycakes.

She doesn't move.

STAR Hell, don't make me get you.

LADY The guy's on his way.
STAR Fuck the guy.
LADY That's your plan? He's here real soon.
STAR He'll be lost.
LADY You know that for a fact, do you, Mr Wise Guy?
STAR Maybe the boys'll eat him.
LADY You know that's not going to happen.

STAR Well, he's no business coming. Did I invite him?
LADY He's just here on business. Your business.

Star's already picked up a shotgun.

LADY That you do not need.
STAR Can never be too goddamn careful, babycakes.

He gets some shells. She knows she can't stop him.

LADY OK, let's suppose. Just suppose.

He starts loading the gun.

LADY What are you planning, honey? To shoot him dead? A real nice friendly desert welcome for a man who's come all this way to see you.
STAR Right between the eyes, baby.
LADY He's a suit.
STAR They're the worst: piranhas in silver thread.
LADY You're funny.
STAR That's why you love me, baby.
LADY He is no piranha.
STAR Then he's a ball-bustin' cock-sucking vampire! That's their whole reason to live, right there! Leeches!
LADY Well maybe you still don't need the gun, honey. The

guy's coming to see you, that's all.

He coughs.

LADY You OK, honey?
STAR You need to undress.
LADY He'll be with us real soon.
STAR Real nice and slow now.

STAR You hear him? No, you don't. He'll be late. Come on, settle me down, baby.
LADY He's never late.
STAR He's never late?
LADY That's his - thing.
STAR That's this guy's thing?
LADY That's his thing, baby.
STAR I don't even know the guy and he's my guy and you know that's his thing?

LADY I met him one time.
STAR You met him when?
LADY Some place. I forget. Some dull party. With you. Don't worry, he's a nobody. Don't you remember, baby? He was the fool kept shaking everyone's hand, saying he was just checking in, all night long.
STAR He was just checking in? What, like a hotel.
LADY That's all he did, baby, all night long.
STAR All night?
LADY He's harmless.

STAR But you know he's never late?
LADY He's famous for it. You met him too, baby. You were there. He's small. Trim. Wears odd socks. Short hair. Sunglasses perched on top of his head. Like a racoon.

STAR Racoons wear sunglasses now?
LADY Just be nice. He's driven a long way to see you.
STAR Where's Stanley?
LADY He works for Stanley.
STAR Could shoot the suit, they wouldn't care. No questions asked: thank you, sir, you did the right thing, another weasel extinguished, here's a medal.
LADY You won't shoot him, honey.
STAR Bury him in the desert, no one'd be any wiser.
LADY Except they know he's coming.
STAR Bury the car. Say he didn't show. Ran off to Europe with some girl. Lit out on the old hippy trail. Met some Indians, took too much peyote, went off the grid.
LADY Don't be crazy, baby. They'd work it out.
STAR So I'd bury him someplace far off. Out by the earth-ships. Put him in the ground real deep.

He laughs. It turns into a wheezing smoker's cough. He stops.

LADY And then you'd walk back through the desert? Covering your tracks? Spraying up dust?
STAR This is what they think of me? They send me the Number Two guy?! No, not the Number two - I hearda him? No! They send me the Number Three. Fuck, he could be Number Four, all I know!
LADY Just see him, baby, hear him out.
STAR They want me dead and buried.
LADY That's not true, they love you, baby -
STAR I wouldn't wish myself on my own worst enemy.

STAR He's never late?
LADY He's building a career, honey. He'd wade through city sewers to beat traffic, stamp on the heads of alligators to

cross the swamp, climb the highest peak in bare feet.
STAR Sounds like a damn fool!
LADY He just needs a nice warm friendly welcome, a cool drink. Give him a moment. Give him time.
STAR Time don't exist in the mesa, baby, just me and you.
LADY You sound like some cheap band after the Bourbon ran out.

LADY You want something to eat? You look awful thin.
STAR Fighting weight.
LADY You sleep last night?

STAR SHRUGS.

LADY Baby, watch my lips: we need a house. This desert dust doesn't do you any good.
STAR Maybe I'll use him for target practice.
LADY No, you won't.
STAR I shot suits in the past.
LADY You winged a man. One time. So they say. And it was some kind of freak accident, from what I heard. You weren't even looking in the right direction.
STAR You don't know, baby.
LADY You are not going to shoot anyone, honey.
STAR Wanna bet?
LADY Just stop -
STAR That he's late.

LADY OK. I'll bet the planes.
STAR You want a plane, it's all yours, give you the keys right now.
LADY The whole collection. I win, they're gone, tear this place down, we get our house.
STAR You want to sell 'em, baby? For the money?

LADY Hell, yes, baby, that's why I came to live with you, right bang in the middle of nothing but desert dust makes you cough and rumpus weed tumbling nowhere. Living in a tin shack. Yes, sir, for your money!

STAR This ain't enough?
LADY You know, honey, maybe I'm just waiting for you to fall down dead so I can run back to civilisation with all your hard earned cash!
STAR Ain't that the truth?
LADY Honey.

LADY Why's it have to be like this?

STAR 'cause I'm old.
LADY You're not.
STAR Older than I thought I'd ever get to see the day. Live fast die young, where'd I go wrong, huh?
LADY You're not old.
STAR Old as the stone hills, honey. Old as this frail land we stand on. Old as the clothes she wore.

He laughs, coughs. She gives up.

STAR Desert dust, baby. If they did their tests, still wouldn't find nothing.
LADY But maybe they could put you back on your feet.
STAR Pump me full of drugs, tell me to move back to the city.
LADY You pump yourself full of drugs.
STAR Different drugs, baby. Different strokes, different folks. You just gotta know how you're primed. What else did the good Lord put us on this earth for?

CANDYLAND

She refers to the shotgun.

LADY Are you putting that thing down? He's on his way.
STAR This old man still got fire and brimstone in his loins, baby, cure all your aches and pains.
LADY You've got a one track mind.
STAR Don't be sore. Come on, bring me all your sweet candy kisses.
LADY I swear to God you'll wear me out.
STAR So the girls say.
LADY Fuck you, cowboy.
STAR OK.

He lays the gun down.

STAR You're gonna lose.
LADY Feels like they're watching us. Like moth balled ghosts. Sad lonely vultures.
STAR Just living the life of Reilly, same as the rest of us.

LADY You're happy, honey, ain't you?
STAR Shit, when've I ever been happier.

He gestures and she starts to unbutton her top. She might put on music, on an old worn cassette machine. He waits for her, enjoying her performance. She may sing along. Slow sensuous teasing. Her top is about to come off.

When they hear ferocious barking.

STAR Fuck. Fuck fuck fuck fuck fuck.
LADY Looks like your boy's not going to be so late.
STAR Fuck!
LADY Think you just lost your planes.

Star checks his watch.

STAR One minute fifteen.

They listen. A car is approaching. The barking continues.

Star picks up the gun.

LADY Baby, no!
STAR One minute five.

They listen as it gets closer.

LADY Honey, you'll confuse him.

But he doesn't put the gun down.

The car is heard pulling up outside, the barking still loud. A car door opens. A voice is heard.

CITY *(outside)* Hi there, folks!
STAR *(hushed)* Fifty three.

Star signals to Lady to keep quiet. Lady shrugs.

STAR He has to step inside.
CITY *(outside)* Anybody home?
STAR Forty two.
CITY *(outside)* Anyone here, sir?

Silence.

Then a car horn is heard.

CANDYLAND

CITY *(outside)* Any person at this place? Hello?
STAR Asshole.

They wait.

Whistling is heard momentarily.

STAR Fifteen.
CITY *(outside)* OK.

Nothing happens.

CITY *(outside)* OK, I am going to be entering the property now, sir.
STAR *(continuing)* Five -
CITY I hope this is not going to be a problem.
STAR Three, two, one -

The man comes in, right on cue.

Immediately Star has the shotgun to his head. The dialogue is fast and furious and overlaps.

CITY Whoa, whoa, what the -
STAR Hands on top of your head!
CITY What the - !
STAR Put your fucking hands on your fucking head, you dumb stupid fuck!
CITY Don't shoot! Don't! Please don't!
STAR Who the fuck are you? You from the IRS? Couple of them buried out back; you from the IRS, you're dead and gone, boy.
CITY I'm not! I'm not from the IRS!
STAR What say we shoot first, ask the dumb questions

later?
CITY I appraised you of my movements, sir. The office notified you!
STAR Don't know you, kid.
CITY We have met, one time -
STAR Down on your knees, boy!
CITY So you don't recall -
STAR What part of kneel do you not understand?
CITY Please, don't do anything fool -
STAR Knees, fuck-wit! Now!

Finally City does so.

CITY Sir, I think this might be - This might be all some misunderstanding, sir. This isn't right, sir, you are under a misapp -
STAR You want me to blow your fucking head off?
CITY Sir!

Silence.

CITY I'll depart, sir.

CITY I am cognisant that this is not a time that is convenient to you.

CITY I do not need to be present at this moment. Sir.

Star holds the gun to the boy's head. City cowers.

CITY God!
STAR You praying, City boy, you come to the wrong place, this ain't no church!
CITY Please!

STAR You made your peace with the good Lord? Maybe you should say your prayers. What you say? Is it worth the risk, going to him without confessing your sins?
LADY Hon.

LADY Hon, maybe that's enough.
STAR Bang!

City hasn't moved.

Finally Star lowers the gun.

STAR OK, kid: who are you?
CITY Harry. Harry Seidler. I mailed you. I work with Stan. Stanley. Mr Kellowitz. In the office, sir. Stanley Kellowitz.

Tense silence.

Then suddenly Star's whole demeanour changes.

STAR Chrissakes, why didn't you say, kid? Hell, you made it! On time too. Pretty damn impressive. *(looking at Lady)* Well, maybe just about one hundredth's of a second late.
CITY Late?
STAR Hey, no need to panic, kid! I won't tell if you don't. Come here.

Suddenly he hauls him up and gives him a big hug.

STAR Welcome to the middle of nowheresville, high under the rainbow cloud. Damn, I was looking forward to shooting you! You ever been clipped, kid?
CITY I figured maybe it wasn't loaded.
STAR Then you figured wrong, boy! Damn, the bullets in

this could rip your head clean from your shoulders, spin you right across the room. Twice! Gun's not a gun 'less it's loaded.
CITY But that's dangerous -
STAR Damn right, boy! Don't mess with the man and the man won't mess with you, ain't I got that figured just about right, honey?

Lady doesn't reply.

STAR So what's the story?
CITY Stanley asked me. To journey out here. To your home.
STAR Bullshit.

Star doesn't speak. City's confused.

CITY You're the prime reason I entered into this business, sir. From when I was young I've always admired you.

CITY Both of you. The Golden Couple. It does not come any better, sir. That I can assure you. I am truly honoured to be here.
STAR Cute kid. OK, so you're what? Eighteen, wet behind the ears, this your first time outside the big city?
CITY Twenty seven years of age, sir.
STAR Jeez. A know-nothing baby!
CITY That's not young. In this business, sir. That's old. With respect, sir.
STAR You call this respect, you see over the dash to drive, who the fuck cares how old you are? You wanna beer?
CITY Not during my hours of employment, no, sir.

STAR Two beers, hon.

LADY Two beers coming up.
STAR You got a problem, City boy?
CITY I don't drink, sir, not while working, that's the truth.
STAR What's the truth gotta do with anything?
CITY Pardon me, sir?

STAR They're not for you.
CITY Sir?
STAR Sweet baby Jesus! Don't call me sir, makes me feel dead and buried. That what you're trying to do, boy? Put me six feet under?
CITY No, sir.
STAR Poison me with a little of your snake charm?
CITY Sir?

STAR You a military kid, City?
CITY No, sir.
STAR Then quit sounding like a toothless prick! Why'd they send you?
CITY Me, sir?
STAR Shit, what's with you? You borrowed one of JFK's brain cells? Wipe it off Jackie O's pretty little dress and keep it all for your lonesome self, did ya?
CITY Sir, I answered this: Mr. Kellowitz – Stanley. He sent me.

Lady's got a six pack of beers out of the fridge, gives them to Star.

LADY Sure you don't want a beer?
CITY No, ma'am.
STAR Think I'm dangerous, watch out for her. Shark with doe eyes. Rip your throat out soon as smile.
LADY Don't believe a word he says, Harry.

A brief look between Star and Lady.

Star takes two beers, chucks the rest back at Lady.

STAR See this?

He turns back to City, shows a scar. Lady takes a beer for herself. They speak at the same time:

STAR (With her bare hands.
LADY (With my bare hands.
LADY You deserved it, baby
STAR Gotta tell it like it is, dude. You trust her, you're a fool. Don't trust her, you're the enemy.

CITY You have access to a telephone, sir? Quick check in to the office and that's me, done.
STAR They don't trust you to wipe your own ass?
CITY I don't set the rules, sir. My cell doesn't work out here, I'd sure appreciate -
STAR Who says there's a phone?

CITY Well, that's certainly a shame for me, sir.
STAR You don't believe me?
CITY I believe you don't have a telephone I can use.
STAR Why'd Stanley send you, kid?
LADY He's not a kid, honey.
CITY Stanley couldn't make it.
STAR Instead he sends a fucking child in diapers.
CITY A Vice President.
STAR Of what? Sunday School?

CITY Excuse me, sir, you don't happen to have a bathroom?

STAR Desert's all yours, kid.
CITY Maybe the house.
STAR What house?

CITY This is where you live? Stanley said -
STAR Change the record, City.
CITY So, this place, everything. It's - ?
STAR Home sweet home.
LADY Wherever he lays his hat.
STAR Not all I lay, is it, baby?
CITY OK.

CITY Sir, well, this is certainly impressive. Isn't it hot? I mean, It must reach - what? 110?
STAR 140 in the shade, you better believe it, boy.

STAR You no likey what you see, City?
CITY Call me Harry, please.
STAR So. City. Tell me what you think.
CITY About this?
STAR Floor's all yours.

CITY It's - it's – original. Authentic. A modern aesthetic sensibility within a native American landscape.
STAR It's an aircraft hangar surrounded by sage brush and dry earth, shit-fucker, spare me the bullshit.
CITY Yes, sir.
STAR This kid for real? Go! Do whatever you have to before you rupture yourself, City.
CITY Yes, sir. Certainly. I'll be right back.

City goes out.

STAR Jesus!

LADY He's not a child.
STAR A piss-in-his-pants baby, who the hell they think I am?

Star goes to the entrance to watch him. Shouts:

STAR Chrissakes, away from the building, kid!
CITY *(outside)* Right, sir! Yes, sir.

STAR That's sacred land! You don't wanna be cursed by no natives, do you?
CITY No, sir!

STAR City, you're standing right on top a nest full of scorpions!

CITY *(outside)* Here, OK?
STAR Wherever you want, kid, don't be shy. Just don't let the bugs bite. One of those nips your pecker, thing'll swell up like a watermelon, damn near explode!
CITY *(outside)* I - I'm just a bit confused, sir.
STAR Just making a little friendly conversation.
LADY Go easy on him, hon.
STAR You know why he's here?
LADY He told you.

STAR *(calling)* Run into any coyotes on the way?
CITY *(outside)* Er… don't think so, sir.
STAR Trust me, you'd know.
CITY *(outside)* Then no, sir. No.
STAR Snakes?

There's no answer.

STAR You know what a snake looks like, kid?
CITY *(outside)* No snakes as far as I know, sir.
STAR Wrap themselves round your axle, you never know. Snakes every which way, lying all over the highway. Like sticks. Force of nature, a snake, goes its own way, crawls in the smallest crack, get just about anywhere it wants, City, remember that. Any rock, you gotta be suspicious. Got one bastard, few weeks back, in the john, sat down, for fucksake, the little fucker's curled under the seat! Sleeping in the shade! Or waiting on me. Didn't wait to find out!

City is back in. He looks for somewhere to wash his hands.

STAR You're a dog marking its territory.
CITY You have water?

CITY There's a john. Full of snakes.
STAR Murderous little treacherous little cold hearted killing bastards.

City still wants to wash his hands.

STAR Water's kinda precious round these parts, City. Nearest well's half an hour, walking.
CITY OK.

City ducks out of the hangar.

STAR Going there on your own? You even know which direction to go?

STAR Watch out for rattlers now! Where the fuck - ?

The opening and closing of a car door.

STAR Not so stupid.

City comes back in with a bottle of water, pours the water on his hands just outside the doorway, finally wipes his hands on his trousers, even if he doesn't want to. It's all quite fastidious. Straightens his tie. Combs his hair.

STAR You better watch out for the tornadoes come through, might make you a mite dusty, boy.

City notices the covered planes properly for the first time.

CITY Pardon me, sir. Are these what I think they might be?
STAR Guess?
CITY How many do you possess, sir? This is an impressive collection. You have a Republic P47 Thunderbolt? P51 Mustang? PT-17 Stearman maybe?
LADY Don't encourage him.
CITY You still here, sweetheart?
LADY Where else would I be if not by your sweet side, hon?
STAR She loves me, don't you, babycakes?
LADY Not as much as you love yourself.
STAR Ain't the only one, baby, what's not to love?

CITY You don't have plans to fly them.
STAR Talk, City. Why not?
CITY Without a landing strip, you have no way to get these airborne.
STAR Damn, how'd I miss that one, City!
CITY My father was a pilot.
STAR Where'd he serve?
CITY Commercial, domestic.
STAR Dullsville! Bus driver in the sky!

CITY Well, that's a point of view, sir.
LADY He's teasing you, ain't you, honey?
CITY I understand that, ma'am.
STAR Hey, tight ass, you'd better watch out! Teasing ain't it, I'm warming for the kill!
LADY Honey, there's no need to be jealous because he knows more about planes than you ever will.
STAR Hush!
CITY She overstates the case, sir. I know the names of one or two planes, my dad was an enthusiast: Hellcats, Tomcats, Wildcats, he knew them all -
STAR OK, kid, I think I know one end of the gearshift same as any man.
LADY Joy stick, baby.

City nods without thinking.

STAR Think I don't know about flying, think you know more'n me?
CITY Sir. I prefer to keep my feet on the ground. If the truth be told.
STAR Maybe I'll shoot you sooner'n I thought.

Star picks up the gun again.

STAR Ten seconds to say something interesting.

Star points the gun at City.

LADY You're not serious, honey.
CITY If they can't land, how did you get your planes all the way out here?
LADY He's not serious.
CITY You couldn't have flown them in. So how would you

do this?
LADY Honey, stop this.
CITY So they didn't fly. They came overland. They rode on trucks.
STAR Think I should bury him in the dirt or just pitch him to the dogs, honey?

Star cocks the trigger.

CITY Stanley had a heart attack.

STAR What?
LADY He's OK?
CITY Stanley's OK, yes, thank you, ma'am. He's a fighter.
STAR When? Bullshit!
CITY Five days ago. He's in the hospital. He has tubes everywhere, it looks worse than it is.
STAR You after his job, City?
CITY Stanley's been good to me, sir.
STAR Stanley's an A1 shit, he ain't good to no one, least of all the creeps and crawlers, the brown-nosed parasites, ain't that the truth?
CITY Stanley's my boss, sir.
STAR Only now he's sick and you're crawling in here all of a sudden like a – like some fucking baby Vice President! But for why, little boy in diapers, you wanna tell me that?
CITY Stanley's got your back, sir.
STAR You scared, kid?
CITY You didn't shoot.

There's the slightest look between City and Lady.

CITY Stanley wanted to tell you himself.
STAR Then mail me the fucking details!

CANDYLAND

LADY Honey, the boy's told you, he did.

CITY They made the journey in crates.
STAR What?
CITY You broke them down. Every single plane. You dismantled the wings. Unbolted the fusillages. Separated the nose cone and tail. Must have been a heavy load. Wide too.
STAR Hey, wise ass!
CITY What a sight that must have been. Trimmed a few cacti, maybe, clipped a Joshua tree or two, rode over a few lazy snakes.
STAR Fucking hey, OK, these dream babies fly.
CITY No one can fault your ambition, sir.
STAR And 'fore you ask, because I can!
CITY That's a hard road. Took me thirteen hours straight.
STAR Takes me eight. Max. On a bad fucking day in a sandstorm so bad you couldn't see the fucking road!

CITY You should come by. Sir, when you're in town. Visit the office. With respect. Everyone would like to see you. You're the man, you're legend, sir. Set a few hearts fluttering.
STAR Tell me something I don't know.

Star points the gun at City.

CITY I've journeyed thirteen hours to help out Stanley who's ill.

CITY You know the hardest part? The hardest part - Was your dogs, sir. Driving past them as fast as I could, I just prayed they were chained. So I wouldn't hit them. I don't like to be late, sir, that's my -
STAR Thing.

CITY Probably got a bark worse than their bite.
STAR Better hope you never find out, kid.
CITY Just put my faith in God.
STAR You a Mormon, kid?
CITY No, sir. Is that important to you?
STAR What're you staring at?

STAR Well?
CITY You don't mind?
STAR Be my guest.
CITY Back in town.

CITY There are rumours.
STAR You hear I got thin? This is fighting weight, kid! Lean and mean.
CITY I didn't hear that, no, sir.
STAR So I'm crazy?
CITY I heard nothing of that nature, sir.
STAR Well, what in hell did you hear?

STAR Real careful, I can smell a lie at a thousand paces: best bullshit detector in the business.

STAR You're a brave little boy, and that's the truth.

STAR Or you're pretending. You hiding something from me, City? Sure hope you cooked up a good story.
CITY Sir, I'm in this place to ask: have you visited a doctor recently, sir?
STAR Crap!
CITY Whether you have seen a medically qualified person in the last month, the last three months, or six, that's my task here.
STAR You have no fucking right!

CITY Or do we need to organise this for you?
STAR (Course I fucking -
LADY (He should be seeing someone.
STAR I see someone, ass-hole!
CITY OK, so the office just needs to know his name. For the record.

City's eyes flick to Lady.

LADY He's not seen anyone. For a long time.
STAR Hey, that's enough!
LADY Just tell the man, why don't you?
STAR Jesus! I see some doctor, he tells me I'm gonna live to a hundred and ninety, la-di-da, course they do, with my money I'm God!
CITY They're just waiting on that final medical report, sir.
STAR So you're a form filler! Petty bureaucracy in the desert. They send me a fucking baby desk clerk!
CITY I am acting to close this thing. If this is impolite in any way, I apologise.
STAR Stanley sends you all the way just to say this? I don't think so. Stanley knows me. Stanley would never be so fucking rude!
CITY We have to be ready, that's all, sir. Rumours make people nervous.

There's a tiny look between City and Lady, almost unnoticed.

CITY The paperwork appertaining to yourself must be delivered in a timeous manner, sir.
STAR I been in this fucking industry longer than you fucking been alive, babyfuckingalligator! Paperfuckingpaperwork! Before you were fucking born, kid!

CITY I understand this, yes sir. I can assure you I have no wish to offend.
STAR Then quit bugging me like - like some tiresome - fucking - maybug!

STAR I'll see the doc. That's what this is about, you want a report, it's done, go home, kid, shame you wasted your time.
CITY Good. Thank you, sir. This will really help, I can assure you.

STAR You done?

CITY You know, sir. You also missed a couple of meetings back there.
STAR Quit while you're ahead, boy.
LADY You missed meetings?
STAR They know me. They got my measurements They know my blood type. They know my muscle to fat ratio. They know my fucking heart beat, for Christ's sake. They been up my ass with their colonoscopy fucking eyes. I'm A1. Fuck's sake, they been in my ear canals, up my nasal passages, that's all this is? This is crap. I'll be there when they need me, not when they want, you hear me! I been doing this thing longer than you been born, boy!
CITY I hear you, sir. And I am relieved.
STAR Well, you tell 'em loud and fucking clear!
CITY I can say this, sir: we are immensely reassured to be fully in possession of these facts, sir.

STAR We?
CITY The company. Desire you to be well.
STAR Don't think you can fool me, kid.
CITY We will supply what you want.
STAR You know what I want, do you?

Star coughs.

CITY That's what I drove out here to discover, sir.
STAR I already got everything!

The coughing gets worse.

STAR Honey -

City passes him his water bottle.

STAR Nothing to worry about. Just running a little low on gas today, baby, that's all.
CITY You need anything?

Star pours City's water out on the floor.

STAR No visitors.

Lady gets water from a faucet, which City hasn't noticed – it's inside the shack. City looks at Star. Star says nothing.

CITY Sir, you rest. Just so much as you need until we call for you.

CITY We're on your side. Five years out, it's not so long.
STAR I'll be there! Ready to tear down the whole goddamn ass-wipe town!
CITY This is good. This I can inform the office. Stan.
STAR You left yet, City boy?
CITY Once the documentation is complete, sir. A few questions, just regular business, then this will be over.

STAR OK.

CITY They're in the car.

City's about to head off.

STAR So tell me: how's he doing? In the hospital.
CITY Mr Kellowitz will bounce back in no time, sir.
STAR I'm gonna shoot you, you don't quit lying to me, City.
LADY Baby, he just wants to help.
STAR Who the fuck are you, City? Tell me why I never forget a face and I don't know you.
LADY You've met him.
STAR We never met, trust me.
LADY You've been out of the loop a long while.
CITY I am sorry I am not memorable to you, sir.

Star coughs.

CITY You need water?
STAR Look like I need taken care of?
CITY Sir, if I may. There's something. I don't understand. You have all your money. Somewhere. In the bank, in funds, this I do not know.
STAR You're speaking out of turn, boy.
CITY The deals Stan's done. You buy planes! Yet you live in a shack. Why? This is not a place of comfort. This is hot. This does not trouble you? Sure it troubles anyone. Your good lady -
STAR You know what's good for my lady?
CITY We'll arrange it, sir. Go to work, find the men, the very best, the company will build you a house. Will complete this house by the time you're back, sir. We'll handle it for you, do everything you need -
STAR You a building contractor now, City?

CITY You both need a house.
STAR I got houses! New York, London, Paris, Rome. Why the hell d'I need more?
CITY OK, sir. This is understood.
STAR You know how much money I got in the bank, do you, City?
CITY That I do not, sir. Only this is not a bank situation. This is about a place for the two of you to live.
STAR Is that so?

Star picks up the shotgun again and points it at City.

STAR Seems all you wanna talk about is money, City. You like the look of that thing?

He points to the safe.

CITY I don't know what that is, no, sir.
STAR You come here, poke around, maybe you are cognisant of the fact I don't trust no banks.
LADY Hon, aren't we a little beyond this kind of crazy paranoia now?
STAR Maybe you heard I don't trust no government neither?
CITY OK, sir, I don't know what we're talking about anymore.
STAR I'm talking about maybe you got two choices. Am I pretend crazy or real crazy? If I didn't shoot you before, Racoon man, maybe that's because I made a mistake!

City flicks a look at Lady. She's impassive.

CITY Sir. I do not know the answer to that question.

Suddenly Star shoots at City. He misses.

CITY Jesus! Jesus!
LADY Hey, hon!
STAR OK, shut the fuck up now!
CITY Jesus, we were just talking only, weren't we? Tell me there's no blood.
STAR Shut the fuck up while I do some thinking, will ya?
LADY He was only speaking, honey.
STAR No more bull! You two keep looking at each other like I'm the only one ain't in the picture.
LADY Honey?
STAR Like you think I'm some old fool.
CITY No, sir.
LADY Baby, quit torturing the poor boy. He's a kid!
STAR Who can look out for himself. City slicker slime boy snake charmer, crawls over alligators to get places, wades through sewers, scales mountains bare foot! Stanley didn't mention no one visiting.
LADY Honey, maybe things have changed; when did you last speak to him?
STAR But that's not what this is, is it?

CITY OK, sir. This is not my place. To talk about your finances, what you need, I understand, truly. Sir, we just want to ensure everything's as comfortable as possible for you. OK. So maybe we started wrong.
STAR Maybe we ain't started 'til I put a bullet through one of your knees.
CITY They said you were dead.

STAR Who did? I'll sue the shit-fuckers!
CITY They said your head was cryogenically frozen. That Stanley was ill. They're twitchy. No one sees you.

STAR You want my business?
CITY You are my business, sir.
STAR Then you follow my rules.
LADY What rules?
STAR Hush now, babycakes.
CITY You want me to live out here, I will do that, sir.
STAR What?
CITY You want me to bring a motor-home, camp out of sight, I'll do that. Arrange someone to fix the place up, get a phone put in, that's all part of the job, sir. Whatever you want.
STAR I want you to sleep naked on the desert floor. Feel your bones sink into the termite dust. Shiver in the goddamn freezing night under the bustling stars. You'd do that for me?
CITY If you want me to do it, sir.
STAR No, I want you to lie cold as a grave, while the scorpions tip toe over your shit-scared little trembling body! Feel the coyotes' foul breath on your weak skin in the pitch black. You ready to do that?
CITY I'll do what it takes, sir.
CITY You ever wake up to a rattler?
LADY Hon, what more do you want from the poor kid?
STAR I want a reason not to shoot.
LADY Because no one just shoots people.
STAR You think I'm no one?

STAR The office even know where you are, boy?
CITY You think I'd leave without them knowing such a thing, sir?
STAR 'Less you weren't never in no office.
LADY We have to keep coming back to this.
STAR Stanley ain't never been here. I like it that way. He knows I don't like visitors. You're the first, now how is that?

CITY I'm honoured, sir.

STAR Wrong answer.

STAR Ain't no map. We ain't on no radar. You don't follow no dancing rain-clouds. How'd you find me, kid?
CITY Few roads in the desert, sir.
STAR I seen you looking at her. Looking at each other, all coochy coo.
LADY Honey don't do this.
STAR I've been watching you two.
CITY Sir, I don't know her.
LADY Baby, you're going stir crazy, maybe we need to get back to some kind of cold reality here.
STAR You don't think this is reality?
CITY I'm here on business, sir. That's all. Your business. On my mother's life. Ask Stan.
STAR You want power of attorney, kid?
CITY (Sorry?
LADY (What?

STAR Punk, you want power of attorney for me, it's simple, just say the word, you got it.
LADY Hon, why are we talking about power of attorney?
STAR You want principal power of attorney, you want durable, we have a witness, I'm of sane mind, you got it right now.
CITY Sir, you don't need power of attorney to be granted to any one person at this time.
STAR You saying no?

STAR Only gotta ask. Always easier to tell the truth than lie, boy.

City's eyes flick to Lady. She's confused.

CITY I am willing to take on the responsibility, sir. If that is what you want. I'd be honoured.
LADY Honey, what's happening?
STAR Can't believe your luck, can you kid?
LADY You'd give away power of attorney to a complete total fucking stranger?
STAR We met him one time.
LADY Don't say such things. Even for a joke.
STAR You think this is a joke?
LADY Stop. Stop this, baby.
STAR Playtime's over, honey. I quit.
LADY What?
STAR Hell, I'm just an old fossil! City boy, you got what you came for, now get out 'fore I change my mind.
LADY Honey, you have no idea what you're doing.

She reaches for him.

STAR Take your fucking, traitorous hands off me!

He throws her away. She falls. She's shocked.

LADY Baby -
STAR City, you need to know what's what, where I keep everything, the combination to the safe where I hold all the deeds, all the information about all the money, everything.
CITY Sir, I didn't come here to cause trouble between you two.
STAR Yeah, well, if it ain't broke, break it.
LADY You're not well.
STAR You, I want gone!
LADY Baby, why are you doing this?

STAR Tomorrow, dawn, you're out!
LADY You don't mean this.
STAR You want me to shoot you too?
LADY You think I care? When you're gone, baby, there's nothing left.

For a moment there's hope. Then:

STAR Please don't say shit you don't mean no more.

He starts to cough.

LADY Honey, please.
STAR Git!

The coughing gets worse. Huge, racking coughs.

Lady looks at City, then goes to Star.

LADY Baby, breathe easy. Come on, baby, come on, breathe real slow.

He tries to shrug her off but he can barely get air into his lungs. City stands seeming fairly helpless, bewildered also.

STAR Water.

Lady grabs the water bottle off City. Star coughs and splutters. They watch in horror as he almost coughs his guts out.

Eventually he calms, but he's a spent force.

LADY I can't see you like this, baby.
STAR Can't bear to see your face no more.

LADY Oh, baby, you don't mean that.

She holds him.

CITY Can I get you anything, sir?
STAR Cream soda.
CITY You got it.

Star starts to laugh, gently, mixed with some dry coughs. City doesn't move.

LADY Baby, you OK?
STAR I'm OK.
LADY That was a rough one. You're gonna be fine. Just fine. That was the pain talking, wasn't it, hon?
STAR Feel like someone punched a spike through my heart.
LADY We'll get you different drugs.
STAR No more.

LADY I'm with you, baby. As long as you want me.
STAR Never wanted you to go.
LADY I'm going no place else.
STAR Not 'til you get my money.
LADY No one wants your money, baby.
STAR Christ, what do I care, I ain't taking it no place.
LADY I love you, baby, you know that. I love you with all my heart.
STAR Join the line, baby. Join the line.

This wasn't what she was expecting. Without thinking she hits him.

STAR Hey, I'm sick!
CITY That's enough!

LADY What do you know?
CITY The man wants me to take care of him, I will fulfil that responsibility. It's my duty to ensure you treat him right, ma'am.
LADY Don't get ahead of yourself, sunshine, I can still shit you for breakfast.
CITY Ma'am, this is not conducive to a peaceful resolution of our situation.
LADY What situation? You have a signed contract with the man, do you?
STAR The man wants a piss.

Star gets up.

STAR Come on, City, let's go hang our cocks to the wind.
LADY Baby?
STAR Ladies not invited. Go on ahead, lover boy.

City is unsure. Star waits.

Reluctantly City walks out first. Star turns and faces Lady.

A silence as he coolly appraises her, then:

STAR Why'd you fuck him?
LADY What? No, baby, I didn't -
STAR Best bullshit detector in the business. *(calling outside)* Wait for me, woncha, lover boy?

Suddenly Star picks up the gun and moves much faster than expected.

LADY Watch out, he has the gun!

CANDYLAND

Star's already outside. Almost immediately there's a bang.

LADY No, baby!

And another shot.

LADY NO!!!

The coyotes howl in the night.

Blackout.

ACT TWO: AMERICAN DREAMER

An empty hangar. No planes yet.

Lady is looking drop dead gorgeous. Star has a kind of low key, rugged perfection. Their tone is light, playful.

Three years before.

LADY Long way from home.
STAR We're here, baby! This is us.
LADY Weekends? Holidays?
STAR Forever and a day.

LADY This place?
STAR Our island hideaway.
LADY If you think this is an island, you're way crazier than I thought, lover boy.
STAR Our desert island heartland.

Star takes Lady in his arms, kisses her.

LADY You are crazy.
STAR Don't want this, we can go back, baby, just say the word. You want those people in your face 24-7?
LADY Did I say that?
STAR You want the fleas jumping your bones, the parasites, whores and petty larcenists?
LADY I do understand, honey.
STAR Losers tagging you like lice, the pimps and rogues, mendicant liars and bitter termites -
LADY That's not what I want!

STAR OK. This is us, baby. Done this for no one else. No one came close, baby. This is my gift to you.

LADY We build a house.
STAR Anything you want, baby, pool, sun deck –
LADY A pool?
STAR You got it.
LADY A barn?
STAR Horses're made for this place, baby.
LADY I don't ever want to be left alone.
STAR Me and you, baby, we're a team.
LADY When you're gone -
STAR I ain't going no place else no more.
LADY One day you'll hit the road again.
STAR Who needs the scramble, baby? A fool game played by no-life pygmies. This is my promise to you.
LADY Just 'cause you catch a mustang, don't make it tame, honey.

Star shrugs.

LADY You're a hard dog to keep on the porch. I have to be clear here.
STAR You know this. Or this is nothing.
LADY Nina must have -
STAR Who's Nina?

LADY I can go back. If this doesn't work. Any time.
STAR You want me to call the lawyers again? What is this?
LADY We none of us like to get lonely, baby.

STAR What are you saying? Are we talking about another person?

LADY There's no one else, baby, you know that.
STAR You do that, anything, you so much as touch another man, I'll bury the fuck!
LADY Great: Neanderthal man speaks.
STAR You want a caveman, I'll act the caveman.
LADY OK.
STAR Just protecting my assets, babycakes.
LADY Don't.
STAR You're gold, you're silver, you're platinum. You're oil to me, baby, blowing up outa the ground. You're rock hard, diamonds, a gleaming universe.
LADY OK.
STAR So don't say any thing else stupid.
LADY What did I say?
STAR Better.

LADY You were married to her for what? Sixteen years. And then?
STAR Before I met you.
LADY You get bored, walk out, is that how it goes? I couldn't do that to another person.
STAR What do you want, baby? This is real. We build our house, the best damn kitchen money can buy!
LADY You want a cook?
STAR We keep it simple, grow our own.
LADY Sounds like hard work.
STAR Then we bring people in.
LADY Which people?
STAR People.
LADY Who'll live with us? Suddenly our desert island is a zoo.
STAR Whatever you want, baby, just tell me what you need to make you happy.
LADY So what do we do? Fuck all day long?

He starts to unbutton her.

STAR Baby, you are way too sexy for your own good.
LADY And when I get old?
STAR You won't never get old.
LADY Where were you?

He continues to undress her.

LADY Did you hear me?

She stops him.

STAR Hey!
LADY You think you just can just disappear and I won't ask questions?

LADY You really think I'm such an idiot?
STAR Hey, let's not break the mood here.
LADY What mood is that?
STAR Babycakes, don't do this.
LADY And don't you ever call me babycakes!
STAR Hey!
LADY I trusted you, shit-fucker, and you do this! This is what you do?
STAR Nothing happened. What happened?
LADY Tell me fairies exist, it'd be more fucking believable!

STAR Sometimes you just gotta trust.
LADY So what are you not telling me?
STAR It's only you now, baby, I swear, on my life.
LADY I can't live here, no.

STAR Baby?
LADY I'm going home.
STAR What home?

This stops her dead.

STAR You walked out on your kids.
LADY I never walked.
STAR Left your butler and your fancy house and the vintage cars parked out front and the nannies and - so don't you ever say it's my fault, OK? It's no one's fault! There is no one to blame here. From where I'm standing. Because you made that choice yourself.

She attacks him.

LADY Bastard!
STAR Hey!

It's a sustained attack, but a bit like a child trying to attack an adult.

LADY I hate you I hate you I hate you I hate you -

He holds her off with his longer reach, makes as sure as he can she can't get his face.

LADY I hate you I hate you I hate you, I hate…

Finally she gives up. She's breathing heavily.

He relaxes for a moment.

STAR You back on the sauce, babycakes?

She attacks him again with a roar of frustration.

And then she gives up.

LADY Some of us like the city, like people. Like to be noticed.
STAR Baby.
LADY I went looking for you. Couldn't move out of the hotel room. I just - wanted you, honey. I couldn't go out, they kept hassling me, taking their shots, flash flash, pushing right in my face, I didn't know where you were! I thought maybe you'd crashed your bike, some place lonely, out on the road. Got in a fight, they left you for dead. Were in some motel room with - I didn't know! People got the room number, the phone wouldn't stop ringing. Creeps. Sickos. I couldn't open the curtains for folk leering with their lenses across the block. I was worried, honey, I needed to see you, just hear your voice. One time only! I could – could only move between the bath and the bed, bath and bed, bed and minibar, minibar and - round and round the room like some sick tiger dying in its cage. You can get sick of room service too, sick of the same drink, the same glass, the same company, the same room, after a while all the waiters just start to look the same, everyone gets a little stir crazy.
STAR You had waiters come into the room?
LADY There were reporters stalking the corridors, honey, didn't I just tell you?
STAR Doesn't need to be like this, baby.

LADY What are you saying?
STAR Eat, drink, make love. It's simple.
LADY Carpe diem.
STAR Now don't go all Miss Harvard brains Latin on me.
LADY Then don't change the fucking subject!

Suddenly he heads out of the hangar.

LADY (*calling after him*) See how quickly you can make a good story, lying's not your strong point, honey, let me tell you!

LADY (*calling*) If you leave, I won't be here when you get back!

LADY (*calling*) You hear me, you bastard?

To her surprise, he does come right back in. He sweeps past her, holding a long cardboard tube.

STAR House.

He opens up the cardboard tube and pulls out a rolled plan. He has nowhere to put it, so he hands her the plans, goes into the shed, comes out with a table top and two trestles, puts up a temporary table (as in Act One), lays out the plan on the top.

LADY You didn't plan on talking to me first?
STAR Surprise.
LADY Maybe I'd like to know what I'm getting into. You vanish into the desert, I think you're dead!
STAR Hell, I'm indestructible, kiddo, you should know that.
LADY Frankenstein's monster.
STAR Trust me, this you'll like.
LADY You just do what you want with no thought for any other person. With no understanding!
STAR All yours, babycakes.

She leans over to have a look. He comes up behind her, looks over her shoulder.

LADY What's this?
STAR Boudoir.
LADY A boudoir!
STAR French.
LADY You think this means brothel, don't you? You think you're building a bordello in the desert?

He points out a different room.

STAR Fishing room.
LADY So where are you going to fish?
STAR We build a pond.
LADY We fill a pond with fish and water?
STAR Tadpoles. Grow into frogs. All kinds of new life here.

He's begun to lift her skirt from behind.

LADY You designed this?
STAR Don't move.
LADY And what's this room? Nursery?
STAR Baby, not now.

He's undone his belt. She stops him.

LADY You made this for someone else.
STAR You!
LADY Nina.
STAR Marry me.

LADY You even divorced?
STAR It's happening, baby. Real soon, just gotta sort out the

paperwork, the lawyer's on it.
LADY Honey, you're like a clown riding a truck with all the wheels off.
STAR You wanna live in town, we'll do that. You wanna move to Alaska, I'll buy you huskies and furs.
LADY You went away for four days straight.
STAR And I'll tell you why. When it's right.
LADY You want to be just like your father? Disappear one day and never come back?
STAR You want your kids? You want me to call the lawyer again; scare your husband.
LADY And when you tire of me, you'll scare me too?
STAR You know that's never gonna happen.
LADY Monster!
STAR Baby, this ain't the place.
LADY What the hell am I doing here?
STAR Hey, that's enough!

He tries to hold onto her, but she escapes his grasp.

LADY Keep your hands off me!
STAR Thousands would kill to take your place.
LADY Fuck you!
STAR Hundreds of thousands.
LADY The number's going up.
STAR And all you wanna do is complain?
LADY You going to stop me?
STAR OK, close your pretty mouth now.
LADY Oh yes, that's more your style, isn't it, Mr. Caveman? Show me how you do it, big boy. Hit me like you hit her!

He comes up to her close.

Face to face. Intense.

STAR Never had a woman as no friend. Didn't think you could til I met you.

Then he kisses her passionately.

Just when she responds, he pulls away, goes over to the sofa. He pummels it, rips off the arm, beats the shit out of it. His actions are filled with rage and frustration, until finally he breaks down crying.

Silence.

A lone coyote howls in the far distance.

LADY He's with you on this one, baby.

She goes to him, he pulls away.

LADY Hey.

He doesn't respond. She smiles.

LADY Babycakes?

Silence.

STAR Think I saw him one time. Some terminal some place. O'Hare maybe. Ready to board a plane. Sure looked like how I imagined he'd be. Same mean far away look in his eyes. Like he saw straight through you. As if there was someplace far off he needed to be, better. Someone he needed far more than - And nothing and no one would stop him. Same hat, I remember that hat, why wouldn't I? Last

thing I remember of him. Back of it as he left mom ready for the nut-house and - Well he never turned back.
LADY I know, baby.
STAR Who'd do that to your own family?
LADY Guess people just get a little confused sometimes.
STAR You're alone and things're done to you and before you know it, you're stealing hub caps, and drunk, and chasing trouble. Orpheus had nothing on him. Never once looked back, the bastard. Not once!

LADY Oh, baby. We'll make it through. Guess I'm blue too. Too many memories. But no more going back, it's gone, your daddy's gone. They can't touch you no more, baby, you're safe.
STAR Never told her how I felt til she couldn't hear me.
LADY She heard you. Don't worry. Even with her eyes closed, even with the drugs, a mother always hears her own son, doesn't she?
STAR Why's it always too late, baby? What's the reason for that? I ask but no one answers.

Silence.

LADY I hear you. Walking in the dark.
STAR Been wrong too many times. Just want to make it right one more time before I go.

He looks at her, then suddenly he's off outside. She doesn't realise at first.

LADY Baby?

He's fast, a car door opens and slams shut outside.

LADY Wait! Take me with you, don't leave me alone! I can't make it without you, baby!

But the engine revs, and he's gone.

Desert silence.

LADY Goddamm!

She comes back in. Coyotes howl in the distance. The sound of a rattlesnake.

She looks at the hangar, vast and empty, kicks one of the doors. The sounds rings, reverberating away into the night.

Where she was perfection, she's now dusty and dishevelled.

She goes to the fridge, opens the door, leaves it open. It's full only of bottles of beer. She takes out a beer, starts to drink, necks it, takes a whole six pack over to the table, opens the next.

She's drawn to the plans. She starts to look at them.

LADY Boudoir.

LADY Fuck. Fuck fucking FUCK!

The sound echoes through the night. She's left on her own a long time, necks the second beer, takes another beer, starts drinking that one. For all her beauty, she's a hard drinker. She studies the plans but doesn't know why: a map of broken dreams

In mid-drink, a car is heard. She waits until the beam of light from the car shines in through the doorway.

And then Star's there, a back-lit god, standing in the doorway.

STAR Can't make it without you, baby.

They stand staring at each other as the lights fade to black.

ACT THREE: AND IN THE END

The Morning after Act One.

There's no sign of anyone in the hangar. Quite a few empty beer bottles strewn around the place.

Something stirs under the table.

City appears out of some kind of bed made out of boxes, with a rope laid round the perimeter. His arm is in a makeshift sling, which has some blood on it, and the rope has caught in his trousers and trails along with him. Bleary eyed, but cautious as he goes, he keeps an eye out for the others. He looks round this space, then in the shack, roots around, finds nothing, comes out, sees the safe. Solid and secure. He heads outside.

As he reaches the doorway, Lady appears from outside. He jumps.

CITY Jesus!
LADY My, aren't you the jumpy one.
CITY He shot me!
LADY You're still alive.
CITY Where is the bastard?
LADY *(seeing his rope tail)* Are you turning into the devil?

She reaches out to untangle the rope from him, he won't let her, pulls it off himself.

CITY You keep away from me.
LADY Not before we talk.

CITY I need to piss.

He pushes past her in the doorway and heads out of the hangar, warily.

Lady enters the hangar, passing him, and we see for the first time quite how tired she is. She has a sore head, cradles a black coffee, which is as strong as she could make it. She sips very slowly.

She looks round the hangar. No sign of life.

She goes over to the plans on the table, looks at them. There's a coffee pot to one side.

LADY Boudoir.

Slowly she pours coffee from her mug all over the plans.

City comes back in, having finished his piss.

CITY Feels like a pack of wild dogs have been gnawing my bones.
LADY It's a scratch.
CITY Coffee?

She points to the shack.

LADY You bring a gun?
CITY Hey, we never said anything about -
LADY What if he tries to shoot you for real?
CITY He won't.
LADY Sure about that?

He heads off into the shack, comes out with milk.

CITY Mugs?
LADY Wash your hands.

He ignores her request to wash his hands, picks up the coffee pot. As there's no mug, he pours the milk straight into the pot.

CITY Well, this is cosy. To the future.

He takes a large swig from the coffee pot, immediately spits it out.

CITY Jeez. It's fulla – fucking mould!
LADY Next time wash your hands.
CITY I need a toothbrush.

He goes to wash his hands under the faucet at last, looks around nervously.

LADY He went off in the truck.
CITY You think I don't know that?
LADY You're lucky he didn't drive over you.
CITY Lucky?

CITY What's the time?
LADY I thought you were the guy with the watch.
CITY It's broke.
LADY 'Bout nine.
CITY Jesus. Jesus fuck!
LADY You expect to be some place else?
CITY You think he'll be back?

He looks at the safe.

CITY He leaves it there. To piss me off!
LADY I don't think it's just for you, honey.
CITY The fucker's laughing at us!
LADY Why did he offer you power of attorney?

CITY I'd take the whole thing and blow it apart, leave right this moment. If I thought there was any way. Lift it on the back of his truck. On the car roof.
LADY Maybe you should have gone to the gymnasium more often as a kid.
CITY Are you laughing at me? Jesus! You bring me all the way to - nowheresville - and then mock me?
LADY He'll be back.
CITY You think he knows?
LADY Hold me.

He doesn't move towards her

CITY You sure he's not waiting somewhere? With his shotgun?
LADY He didn't shoot you last night.
CITY He shot me!
LADY Steve, he didn't shoot you, trust me.
CITY Maybe he can't shoot straight. Maybe he's too drunk or full of drugs. You got a bathroom? I feel sullied and bloodied.

CITY Don't worry, I don't expect a yes.

He goes over to her and kisses her. She slaps him. Hard.

CITY Fuck's that?

He doesn't fight back.

CITY You have any idea how beautiful you are? Come back with me to LA right now, find some place to live that's proud to be covered in asphalt.
STAR Still here, City?

Star stands in the doorway. He's a mess, bloody from head to toe, as smashed up as you can be and still able to walk. He's barefoot, his feet are black. He has the shotgun cradled in his arms

LADY Baby.
STAR Don't move.

LADY What - happened?
STAR Smashed the truck up some place, some hole, some rock, what d'I know, just wanted to fly above this cripple land, baby, couldn't get no levitation.
LADY Oh, hon.
STAR Damn thing had a little party up a tree.
LADY Oh, baby, come here, baby.
STAR Keep away from me.

LADY Just let me see -
STAR Maybe busted a rib, maybe two, who knows, this old body's been patched up more times 'n - more times 'n – Gimme a beer, would ya, City?
LADY Take your shirt off, baby, let me see the damage.
STAR Don't get all sexy on me, we got company.
LADY Take off your goddamn shirt!
STAR Which I would if I could lift my arm.

She goes close, starts trying to get his shirt off. He holds on closely to the gun.

LADY Jesus, you're a mess!

Star pushes Lady away.

STAR Where's that beer?

Star faces City with the gun.

STAR Got a real mean streak in me, City; so far I've been a pussycat.

City goes to get the beer.

Star takes the bottle, necks the whole thing without stopping. Lady grabs one for herself too. It's combative.

CITY Shouldn't we get him to the doctor?
STAR Think I burnt my feet. Made a bonfire, walked across the gleaming hot embers in the dawn, clear my thoughts.

He sees the coffee dripping off the table and the architectural plans.

STAR You two fight?

STAR So anyone want to tell me how this thing ends? What we have here?
LADY Baby, it's nothing, this is our desert island, our heartland.
STAR This the end of our dream? All holed up in no place like home, crazy as a lynx, some new Howard Hughes drowning in dust?
CITY You tried to shoot me.
STAR That's right, City. So you know how crazy I am yet?

LADY I never slept with him, baby.
STAR What d'you say, City? You agree?
CITY Nothing happened.
LADY It's all in your head, baby.
STAR That's right! Except. This little plot! Which one of you clowns thought up that? What were you gonna do, tie me up, scare me a little? Tie her up too, pretend you weren't in this together?
CITY You offered me power of attorney, sir, I have no reason to steal from you.
STAR Who the fuck asked your opinion, City?
LADY You want coffee?
STAR You wanna bury me in the desert, be my guest.
LADY This is such horse manure!
CITY She loves you, sir, I am 100 per cent certain of that fact.
STAR My whole life'd be better, I believed you.
LADY Baby, let's get you to a hospital.
STAR And I'm fixing breakfast. You want waffles? Last chance saloon.

Lady gives City a look to say 'Don't take the bait'.

CITY *(saying no)* Only with syrup.
STAR Where the fuck would I get maple syrup in the middle of the fucking desert, City?
CITY That's what I was -
STAR Course there's fucking maple fucking syrup!
CITY OK.
LADY He burns them.
STAR I do not.
LADY You burn waffles like you crash automobiles, honey.
STAR Maybe 'cos I like 'em crisp! City?
CITY OK. I'll take my chances.

STAR Two fresh waffles coming up.

He disappears inside the shed. The other two talk very quietly.

CITY What do we do?
LADY You're doing just fine.
STAR *(calling)* TALKING ABOUT ME OUT THERE?
LADY TALKING ABOUT NOTHING, HONEY.

She's about to say something else to City, but gets a warning look from him as Star puts his head out.

STAR Speaking pretty damn quiet for talking 'bout nothing.
LADY We were discussing you going to the hospital.
STAR Bullshit! Never felt so good. You sleep well, kid? Tell you, was tempted to put a rattler inside the rope, just to see the two of you snuggle up real close.
LADY You were here?
STAR Wanted to make sure you weren't planning on going no place without me.
LADY Hon, you know I wouldn't.

Smoke has started coming out of the shack

STAR Fuck!

Star races back in, and we hear him from the shack

STAR Fuck, fuck, fuck, fuck, fuck!
LADY Warned you.
CITY Do we help?
LADY He likes to swear in the kitchen. *(Calling)* That's his thing!

STAR Fuck, fucking burnt fucking fuck!

Star comes out through clouds of smoke with blackened waffles. But he's upbeat.

STAR Waffles for two. Reformatory style.
LADY Think you need to get yourself a smoke detector, honey. You come out of there like you're in some kind of war zone.
STAR I love the smell of waffles in the morning.

Star slaps the burnt waffles down on the trestle table. City is about to eat when he's stopped.

STAR For what we are about to receive, may the Lord make us truly thankful. Amen.

City starts eating. Star watches.

STAR You start something, you're gotta finish.
CITY It's good.

City struggles, but he's starving. Lady has another beer. Star stops her without even looking.

STAR That's enough. Honey?

She ignores him, drinks her beer deliberately.

City finishes his waffle, semi-triumphant.

CITY Done.

Star tosses his own waffle in the bin, plate and all.

STAR First rule of life. Don't eat no reformatory chow. Never know what they put in it. So you wanna know what happened? Or you just too polite to ask?

LADY You hit a tree, honey, it happens every time you go in something that's faster than you.

STAR Hey, you have to choose to hit a tree in the desert. It's a choice!

LADY And I thought it was a plain and simple death-wish.

STAR Just a shame I had no passenger, ain't it?

City and Lady look at each other, a flicker, and then back to Star.

CITY You try to kill yourself in the desert, there's a reason.

STAR You think I give a shit what you think, City?

CITY My mom died when she was twenty seven. I was five years old. They ripped out her womb, took away one of her - her left mammary, my daddy said. But still they couldn't save her. She turned yellow. Beneath the skin, that's what I remember.

STAR I weep for you, City boy.

CITY Whoever you think you were. Whatever special claim you think you have to this earth. I see you.

STAR Well, don't you have the big, dangling, clanking scary old elephant balls all of a sudden, City?

LADY Honey?

Lady's waiting for an answer.

CITY You haven't told her.

STAR Hell, the Lord Almighty's hand done reached down, ain't that a pisser? This what you came all the way for, City? The circus finally coming off the road, they won't be putting up those old canvas tents much longer, no siree.

CANDYLAND

LADY Baby?
STAR Cancer. Non operative.

Lady is stunned.

STAR What's the matter, ain't we in Kansas no more?
LADY Baby, I didn't know.
STAR *(to City)* This what you wanted?
CITY I swear to God, I'm as sorry as you about this, sir.
STAR Don't call on no God, City, 'less you want him to strike you down for being one lying sonofabitch!
LADY I'm sorry, baby.
STAR Good. Everybody's sorry. Except me. Who's fucking delirious! OK, let's cut to the chase. Prognosis: one day at a time, that's it.
LADY No!
STAR That's what the doc put in his last report. Did all the tests too. First one was two, nearly three years back.
LADY You've known this thing three years?
STAR Gave me two months to live, I'm a walking miracle!
LADY Oh no.
STAR Don't want no drugs, don't want to die like a dog, don't want no chemo. I don't want no one to remove no tumours, don't want no surgery.
LADY No, you're wrong, baby, no, we'll go see someone. Someone new!
STAR One time, in the desert, and there's a double rainbow in the sky. I ain't never seen anything so beautiful in my whole life. Like a vision. Just for me. Never felt such peace. Never felt the land so strong beneath my feet. And then the rain falls. Batters me, I am baptised anew, like a blessing. Only turns out there's been a fire. Los Alamos Nuclear Labs has a small problem, only they're so clever they don't tell no one. And I'm the damn fool sitting under the rainbow cloud,

letting all that beautiful multi-coloured radiation purify me.
CITY You're saying that's what caused it? That's a suit right there.
STAR Life caused it! That's it! You're here and then not. That's what happens, make the most of it. You look for love and trust and joy and respect and loyalty 'cos otherwise – otherwise your beautiful rainbow's just fulla poison.

STAR Well, sure looks like I ain't gonna be working on Maggie's farm no more, City, how'd you like that? Go tell Stanley.
CITY That's not important at this moment, sir.
STAR No, City? Why not?
CITY Sir?

STAR 'Cause Stanley knew months ago. You think I'd let them see me like this?
LADY Baby, Stanley knew and I didn't?
STAR Still want your power of attorney, City?
CITY Sir, maybe Stanley didn't communicate all this information to me, but we want to help you in any way we can, sir.
STAR Then make these babies fly.
CITY I'll send down an engineer soon as I get back, sir.
STAR Now.

CITY You want me to put them in the air now, sir, or start the engines over? You have no runway.
STAR The whole desert's a damn runway, City, you never look? Best goddam strip in the world, salt flats, the rain comes, smoothes them like – like ice. Fly in over the mountains, it's all yours!
CITY You have gasoline? No, sir, I haven't seen any tanks.
STAR Then you don't get power of attorney.

CITY OK, this we'll do. We'll get you gasoline, lay down tar if need be. You've got enough money, we can do whatever you want. You want a doctor with a second opinion? There will be other drugs
STAR You a drug dealer as well as a realtor now, City?
CITY We'll get you nurses too, sir. A team of people to take care of you.
STAR What are you scared of, City?
CITY Whenever you want, sir. Wherever. We'll get you the best care humanly possible!
STAR I got care!! Hell, my old lady's gonna look out for me.
CITY Not on her own, sir.
LADY Who says she will?

STAR You won't care for a dying man?
LADY I've been caring for a dying man for two, near three years maybe, only some damn fool forgot to tell me! Maybe it feels like I've just about done my time.
STAR Don't tell me this is all about one lousy fucking safe.
LADY This was never about a safe.

STAR So why's he keep looking like the thing might jump up and bite his ass?
LADY Stop now, you're only hurting yourself, baby.
STAR What the hell did you tell him?
LADY I love you, baby, I wouldn't harm you.
STAR You wanna bust my balls? This thing gives you carte blanche to fucking open me up like some giant fucking scar?
LADY Don't do this -
STAR This is nobody's business but mine! And I am a healthy man. I am a walking prince. I am a living fucking miracle. I'm gonna lick this thing. I am a survivor! I am gonna beat this shit even if it kills me!

CITY Which it will, sir, trust me. Soon. By your colour now this is clear to me.

STAR That what they teach you at snake charm delinquent school, kick a man when he's down in the dirt? Tell me what I got to lose, City, I shoot you right now?

LADY Oh, honey, I'm sorry.
STAR You sound like a Catholic, say sorry enough times and the whole world's meant to fall at your pretty little feet in forgiveness, is that it?
LADY I thought this would be - we'd be different.
STAR Fighting stock, baby, how could I be any different? And you failed the test.
LADY The test?

LADY No, baby.

LADY You knew? You did this thing, knowing?
STAR You wanted my money, you just had to ask. City gets power of attorney, you trust him?
LADY He isn't anything.
STAR Shoulda thought of that before you made your pact with the devil.

LADY You didn't need to test me, baby.
STAR You slept with him.
LADY You slept with every fucking woman this side of the Ocean!
STAR Not any more, baby. Not since you. Nope, you were all.
LADY Like a leopard changes its spots.
STAR This one did, baby. Painted over the spots, become a new animal. Stayed on the porch in his rocker.

LADY Bullshit.
STAR I'm old, baby, tired; outa gas.
LADY That's meant as a compliment to me?
STAR Believe me, that's the best I can give.
LADY Well, maybe. Maybe it's just not enough. You were gone. Without a word.
STAR Stanley told me to go see a doctor.

STAR Sometimes - sometimes it's the simple things. Saw the doc, then. Got on my bike and rode clear through the desert, just - just clearing my head. Came back to the hotel and - you were changed, baby.
LADY You knew! When we first came here. The very first time.
STAR Told you lady. Best bullshit detector in the business.
LADY Why didn't you say?
STAR You broke my heart, baby, just tryna see if it could be fixed one last time.

LADY You don't think I gave up everything?
STAR Didn't give up your kids, honey, don't fool yourself. They threw you out; didn't want no old boozer sliding down the walls with no bottle in her hand, wondering where in hell she was.

She's shocked by this, numbed

LADY I do not - I am not a drunk.
STAR All in the court testimony, baby. Why else'd they give custody to that mean little prick of a husband of yours?

She's holding a bottle. It looks like she's going to hit Star with it. Instead she suddenly hurls it away to smash in the darkness.

LADY And you are the single most cruel man I have ever met.
STAR Just looking for the ultimate high which you ain't never gonna get cos it don't exist, baby! I know! I am beyond the grave, I am past this fragile land. I know! No such place!
LADY No!
STAR Just telling the truth, baby. That's love, no place to hide.

He moves to her, leaves the gun.

STAR First time ever I saw you. Very first. I knew. That's all it was, would be. You. Your hair in the sunlight, your smile, eyes. Glowing. With life and joy and - and hope. Vitality. And truth. Don't know why, baby. And don't know why you and no one else. You'd have to ask the Lord. Ain't we all the same? Heads and arms and legs and - And then there's love at first sight, and then there's the soul, that's what it is.
CITY Sir, it's time you were setting down your last will and testament.
STAR What are you, lawyer too? So who is this guy? Some fucking dumb waiter?
CITY Let's just get the money and leave.
STAR You're a pretty cocky young fellow ain't you, City?
CITY You shot me. You forfeited all rights when you did that. I either take the money now or we meet in court and I take you for fucking millions.
STAR Maybe I should shoot you right next time.
CITY I've got your gun.

City's holding it.

CANDYLAND

STAR Ain't you the clever one?
CITY I like to think I'm not stupid. I'd like to be the nice guy but I'm not. I feel no pity. You had everything and you - you chose to play games. All this, here. It's bullshit!
STAR So you bring him all this way for - For what? Baby, you can do better than this sleaze-ball. Call an Attorney, you're so angry. Think you can force me to sign anything? What if I just don't care?
CITY We can do what we like to you. Tie you up. Torture you. Leave you to the scorpions, to the coyotes, watch them rip you apart piece by piece. Chop your fingers off one by one. Pop out an eyeball, you'll sign anything we say.
STAR You'd do that? For him?

LADY Let's just not do anything stupid.
CITY The guy's a walking corpse, didn't you hear him?
LADY I don't want it to end like this.
CITY Anything he says, it's ain't worth the paper they wrote him on. Love at first sight, it's a line!
STAR Lemme tell you something, boy -
CITY No! I've had enough of listening to your voice. Yabbering - gibbering! - telling us you're special. Well, you're not. You're just one small speck of humanity the same size as anyone else, just a loser who got lucky. You coming?
LADY We can't just leave him.
STAR I had you nailed, boy. From the very first.
CITY You don't think he's happier than he's ever been? He wants to die in the desert. Christ's sake, he crashed into the only tree in the whole damn landscape, you don't think that's a death-wish right there?
LADY He's in pain.
STAR Leave, go see your kids, baby, enjoy your life.

LADY Maybe I will.
STAR Do it. Hell, if it gets you what you think you want.
CITY We'd like it if you opened up the safe, sir. We need to be on our way.

STAR Why him?
LADY I thought you were with some woman. I swear I never - I wanted - to hurt you back, baby, the only way I knew how.
STAR I told you.
LADY Hell, I didn't know! I just wanted a house! And - and a nursery. Kids! To be happy. Not some test! Not some stupid fucking test!
CITY OK, we need to access this safe, sir.
LADY Why don't you just shut the fuck up?
STAR That cheap fake shit on your boy's wrist. Soon as I saw that thing, I knew.
LADY I lost you someplace.
STAR Who calls Stanley Stan? No one. And Stanley don't bounce, kid! He's a sloth, ain't that the truth? With mean eyes and a heavy gut. A fat lard-ass with clogged arteries who smokes Cuban cigars.
LADY You can't just die!
STAR So go home, take that faggoty-ass pussy whipped retard pretend office boy lawyer with my blessing.
CITY OK, what's the combination to this thing?
STAR You want to hear my last words first?
LADY Don't say that, baby.
CITY OK, cut the crap, OK?
STAR Do not go in there if you value your life.
CITY Is that a threat? Boo fucking boo! You think you can scare me? We hold all the cards. Your power of attorney won't be worth the paper it's writ on, we all know that. So we finish this thing now.

CANDYLAND

City is pointing the shotgun straight at Star's head

STAR Oh Lord, I'm all a-fearful!
CITY You praying? You're in the wrong place, this ain't no church.
STAR Save the poor white trash sinners from themselves, Lord. They know not what they do.
CITY The number.
STAR You have my advice.
CITY Well maybe you've given enough fucking advice for one lifetime!
STAR You wanna open it up, go ahead, City. Code's on the wall.
LADY No.
STAR Always has been, always will be, baby, been waiting for you all along. Ain't no secrets from you, baby. And the Lord said let there be light.

City thinks it's a trick, watches suspiciously as Star moves over and turns on the shack light switch.

The shack lights up. There's writing on it.

STAR Think I'd remember all those numbers? Only gotta look and the good Lord will guide you.

City goes to the safe.

STAR Maybe you don't deserve - Maybe under that - all that heart-stopping beauty and fine bones and Harvard Latin brains, they got you mixed up with someone else at birth, baby.

Lady reads the code to City.

LADY 21 left, then 32 right.
CITY OK.
LADY 13 left on the second dial, on the red dial.
CITY I got it already.
LADY 12 right on the green.
CITY Yup, I'm there.
LADY 7 left -
STAR It's open.
LADY Don't trust him!

But City tries it. The door opens. City leans in, stops, is suddenly very still.

CITY Fuck!
LADY What's that?
STAR This I gotta hear.
CITY Fuck.
LADY What?
STAR Don't do it, City.
LADY What's going on?
STAR Man got himself a real nice leaving present.
LADY What the hell are you talking about?
STAR Shh, baby. Want the package, just gotta pass a little test, that's all.

Lady heads for the safe, she can't see what's going on behind its open door.

STAR Stop.
LADY What's in there?
STAR Might want to pay attention now.

Lady stops.

STAR Them things move faster than your brain thinks, City. He can feel you breathe. Near as dammit hear your sweat. One of them bites, you don't get to the hospital fast enough, trust me.

STAR Fool brought it in his automobile, kind of fitting. Found it while poking round last night, see what kind of man we're dealing with. A fool who hoards Hershey bars in the trunk of his car. In the desert, Steve!
CITY Harry.
STAR Never try to hustle a hustler, boy, it don't work. I was born hustling, how'd you think I got to the top of the whole goddamn insanitary heap?
CITY He's moving.
STAR He's watching you move.

Neither Star nor Lady move.

STAR Sorry, would help, but got me a busted arm. Don't do anything fancy or the good Lord will make of you a dead man, that I can assure you.
LADY OK, that's enough.
STAR You hear that, lover boy. Sounds like my good lady won't ride to the rescue. Turns out I was mistaken. Shows how wrong a man can be when he's blinded by love.
LADY I said that's enough!

She hits Star with a bottle straight across the head.

STAR Fuck!

He crashes to the floor. At the same time, City pulls his hand back fast.

CITY Fuck, he bit me!
LADY No one bit you.
CITY Bastard fucking bit me! What the fuck happened? What the fuck just happened? Fuck! Fuck!

Lady's looking for something to get the snake with, finds a wrench, starts creeping towards where it's hidden behind the safe.

LADY Put your arm level. Keep still. Lower your blood pressure.
CITY My blood pressure's through the roof!
LADY Keep calm.
CITY How can I keep fucking calm? Am I dying? Is this dying? How long does this thing take? Why don't I know anything?
LADY Can you feel it?
CITY I can feel it.
LADY If you can feel it, that's good. Keep feeling!

Lady suddenly hits out at the snake with the wrench, pummels it.

LADY Gotcha!
CITY I'm gonna die?
LADY Chrissakes, suck out the wound. You seen TV. Tie a ligature.
CITY It works?
LADY Fuck should I know, that's what they do!

She lifts the snake, bloodied and crushed, throws it out of the way, reaches into the safe for the envelope. City starts licking his wound, spitting out the venom.

LADY You won't die. He's lying. Damn thing ain't poisonous, sure, how d'you think he put it there, he'd be dead too.

Star is coming to. His head hurts.

STAR You watch too many movies.
LADY Guess it gave me something to do when I got tired listening to your voice, honey.

City staggers momentarily.

CITY Don't feel so good.

City suddenly heads outside.

Lady barely notices him go as she rips open the envelopes.

LADY What is all this crap?
STAR Love letters.
LADY Love letters! Where's the money? Where're the title deeds? Where's - Something I can own for myself!
STAR Thought you did it all for love, baby.
LADY Love needs to eat.
STAR All the candy you could handle, still wasn't enough.
LADY Too much candy rots your teeth.
STAR You broke my heart, baby.
LADY Stop this, OK! This is such a load of horse-manure!
STAR Imagine it was true. And you threw all that away.
LADY What's the difference? What would I have anyway? Memories?
STAR I'm sick, baby, no more games. I left the whole thing

to you, long ago. You're a rich girl, don't spend it all on booze.
LADY What else is there?
STAR Find a new way to fly.
LADY And if I never loved you?
STAR Don't matter a damn. I loved you, that's all that matters, ain't nothing you can do with love than give it.
LADY Oh, baby.

She comes over to him. She holds him in her arms.

STAR All I wanted, just you and me, here, nothing else. Just a little peace 'fore the black hours. Just a little beauty as the sun falls below the horizon.

Suddenly City comes roaring in.

CITY Bastard!
LADY What?
CITY He slashed the goddamn tires!
LADY So put on the spares.
CITY All of them!
LADY You didn't think?
CITY So we got no truck, a sedan with no tires.
STAR And Hershey bars melted all over the trunk, ain't life a bitch?

Suddenly City pulls out a pistol.

CITY Murdering lying fucking cunting bastard!
LADY No!
STAR Roll 'em, kid, I'm -
CITY Bastard!

City shoots Star. Blood. Star is knocked back.

STAR Ready.

City himself staggers.

LADY No, baby.
CITY I'm going to die! Because of him! Because of this!
LADY We are not going to die. No one is going to die!
CITY What do I do?
LADY Baby, hold on, baby.
CITY What do I do?
STAR Wanted to. Believe in.
LADY What did you say? You say something, honey?
STAR World got…
CITY This cannot be happening.
LADY Baby, no, keep talking.
STAR Greedy.
LADY It all gets to so you don't know.
STAR Gotta be…
LADY Which way is up or down.
STAR Who you are.

Star slumps.

CITY He's dead?
LADY There's ways. There's got to be ways.
STAR Baby -
LADY Oh, baby, I did love you. I do. Still love you.
STAR White lie. For the dying.
LADY What if it's true?

City begins to shiver with cold in the sweltering heat. Lady continues talking and trying to resuscitate Star.

LADY Come on, come on now, baby, hold tight to me.
CITY Can't feel my arm.
LADY Baby I love you, don't leave me, baby don't leave me, I love you, please, come back to me, baby, come on, don't go, baby, come on.
CITY Can't feel anything.
LADY Come back, baby, I love you.
CITY I can't feel.
LADY Come on!!

Star dies in her arms.

CITY Pity. Like to have danced on his grave.

City collapses. He's still alive, but on his way out.

LADY No, baby.
CITY Can't feel can't feel can't feel can't feel can't feel can't feel can't feel can't feel…

City gets quieter and quieter until he stops. Lady weeps as she holds Star. City stares out unseeing. Lady tries to pull Star tight to her, hold him closer, but he's a dead weight.

Quiet.

Then the light builds. Soon it's pouring in through the hangar doors as the roar of old planes fills the air, and builds to a thundering crescendo.

Then all is silent again.

Lady is left alone with the two dead men.

CANDYLAND

In the distance a lone coyote howls.

As the lights fade.

Ends

ALSO BY JEREMY RAISON

THE RAIN GATHERING
Two actors (1m, 1f)
A twenty something man and woman meet at the tail end of their relationship. The story of their doomed love affair is revealed in flashbacks. This award-winning experimental play was a big hit when first performed at the National Theatre, the Traverse Theatre and on Radio 4.

THERESE RAQUIN
Five actors, (3m, 2f), optional chorus
Zola's classic tale is given a thrillingly theatrical treatment in a version that was acclaimed on its premiere at Glasgow Citizens Theatre. Therese is already married to her sickly cousin, Camille, when worldly Laurent is invited into her home. Murder brings Laurent and Therese together. It also tears them apart. Zola's novel has been much imitated, but never bettered.

WAKE ME IN THE MORNING
Three actors (2m, 1f)
The most famous actress in the world. The most powerful man. A brutal battle of the sexes leads to tragedy. Shades of Marilyn Monroe and J. F. Kennedy in this acclaimed stage play premiered in Glasgow at Oran Mor's A Play, A Pie and a Pint in 2014.

BRING ME SUNSHINE
Four actors (2m, 2f)
Eric isn't feeling well. He feels even worse when he realises Ernie is doing a funeral oration for him. Carol just wants her husband back, but doesn't know how. Angie tries to help as her own life falls apart. A moving comedy full of magic and wonder, about friendship, love and loss, featuring two men who may or may not be Eric Morecambe and Ernie Wise.

THE SOUND OF MY VOICE
Two actors (1m, 1f)
Morris Magellan is a successful executive, but he has a problem. He is a chronic alcoholic. Ron Butlin's classic novel was adapted with great success for the Citizens Theatre and subsequently chosen by Made In Scotland to represent the best of Scottish work at the Edinburgh Festival,

CANDYLAND

receiving 4 awards and seven 5 star reviews.

www.ingramcontent.com/pod-product-compliance
Lightning Source LLC
LaVergne TN
LVHW051705080426
835511LV00017B/2748